CW01308317

A Book About Fennec Foxes
AMAZING EARTH: Wild Animal Facts
Written and designed by Dawon Seashore

COPYRIGHT © 2022 by Dawon Seashore

All rights reserved.
No part of this publication may be reproduced, stored in a retrieval system, stored in a database and / or published in any form or by any means, electronic, mechanical, photocopying, recording or otherwise, without the prior written permission of the publisher, except in the case of quotations embodied in critical reviews and certain other noncommercial uses permitted by copyright law.

Information contained within this book is for entertainment and educational purposes only. Although the author and publisher have made every effort to ensure that the information in the book was correct at press time, the author and publisher do not assume and hereby disclaim any liability to any party for loss, damage, or disruption caused by errors or omissions, whether such errors or omissions result from negligence, accident, or any other cause.

Dawon Seashore

A Book About Fennec Foxes
FOR KIDS

Dear reader,

We are happy to present to you A Book About Fennec Foxes. This book is part of our Wild Animal Facts series where we take a look at some amazing facts about Earth's many fascinating animals.

The book was created for all youngsters out there, and any curious adult, who love to learn more about their favorite creatures.

We sincerely hope you enjoy and have fun reading. After, you can find out if you learned something new in a fun quiz at the end of the book. There are lots of beautiful photos as well!

Be sure to leave a review to let us know how you liked the book. It helps a lot to improve and expand on future publications.

Sincerely yours,

Wild Animal facts Team

Dawon Seashore

A Book About Fennec Foxes

FOR KIDS

Dear reader,

We are happy to present to you A Book About Fennec Foxes. This book is part of our Wild Animal Facts series where we take a look at some amazing facts about Earth's many fascinating animals.

The book was created for all youngsters out there, and any curious adult, who love to learn more about their favorite creatures.

We sincerely hope you enjoy and have fun reading. After, you can find out if you learned something new in a fun quiz at the end of the book. There are lots of beautiful photos as well!

Be sure to leave a review to let us know how you liked the book. It helps a lot to improve and expand on future publications.

Sincerely yours,

Wild Animal facts Team

TABLE OF CONTENT

What are they?	7
How big are they?	9
What do they look like?	11
Where do they live?	15
What do they eat?	16
Daily Life	19
Living in the Desert	20
Behavior	23
Family Life	27
Communication	29
Interesting Facts	30
Lifespan	33
Fennec Foxes as Pets	35
Future of Fennec Foxes	37
Quiz Time!	38
Glossary	41

SCIENTIFIC NAME: *Vulpes zerda*
The fennec fox is a small creature named after the Arabic word for fox: **fanak** or **fenek**.

Also known as the desert fox, the fennec fox is best recognized by its large, oversized ears that point upward!

The ears of a fennec fox are very large compared to its body unlike, for example, ears of a red fox.

Red fox

WHAT ARE THEY?

Fennec foxes are **mammals*** which means they have fur and feed their young with milk.

They are a small **species** of foxes (family Canidae) found mostly in the sandy deserts of North Africa.

*if the words in **green** are a bit hard for you to understand, look up what they mean in the glossary at page 41-42

Fennec foxes are the smallest living canid species!

Chihuahua

CANID - an animal of the dog (Canidae) family

They are similar in height and length to Chihuahuas – the smallest dog breed, but the ears and tail take up much of a fennec fox's size... Its body is smaller than a chihuahua's.

Did you know?

The Canidae family includes dogs, wolves, foxes, jackals, dingoes, and other dog-like animals.

Jackal  Grey wolf  Dingo

8

HOW BIG ARE THEY?

Male fennec foxes (reynards) and females (vixens) are hard to tell apart, but reynards are a about heavier.

14 – 16 in

7 – 12 in

Fennec foxes are 14 – 16 in (35.5 – 40.5 cm) long. Their tail adds 7 to 12 in (18 to 30 cm) in length.

Their impressively long ears point up 4 – 6 in (10 to 15 cm) in length.

Females usually weigh around 2 lb (0.9 kg) while males weigh up to 3 lb (1.4 kg).

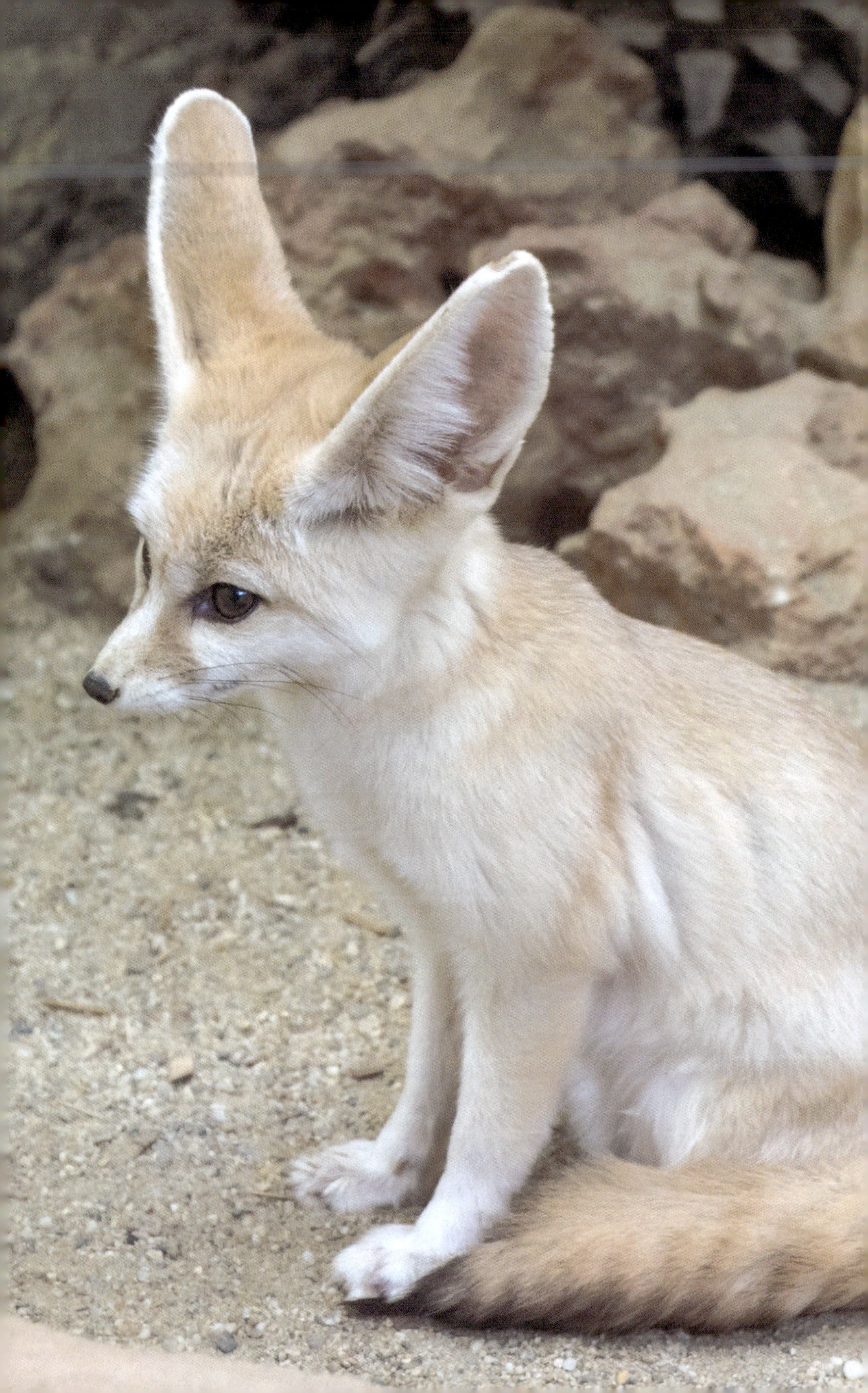

WHAT DO THEY LOOK LIKE?

A fennec fox has a tiny body with short legs.

It has light, sandy-colored fur which serves as camouflage, hiding the fox while out on the sand.

bushy tail with black tip

It has fur on the soles of its feet that allows it to walk around on hot sand without a problem!

11

Did you know?

Fennec foxes have long and sharp, **curved claws** that help them dig their burrows with great speed!

Fennec foxes have large, bat-like ears.

Big-eared bat

Their large eyes and small noses are black.

However, this one's eyes are closed because it is sleeping... shhh! Let's not wake it and move on to the next page.

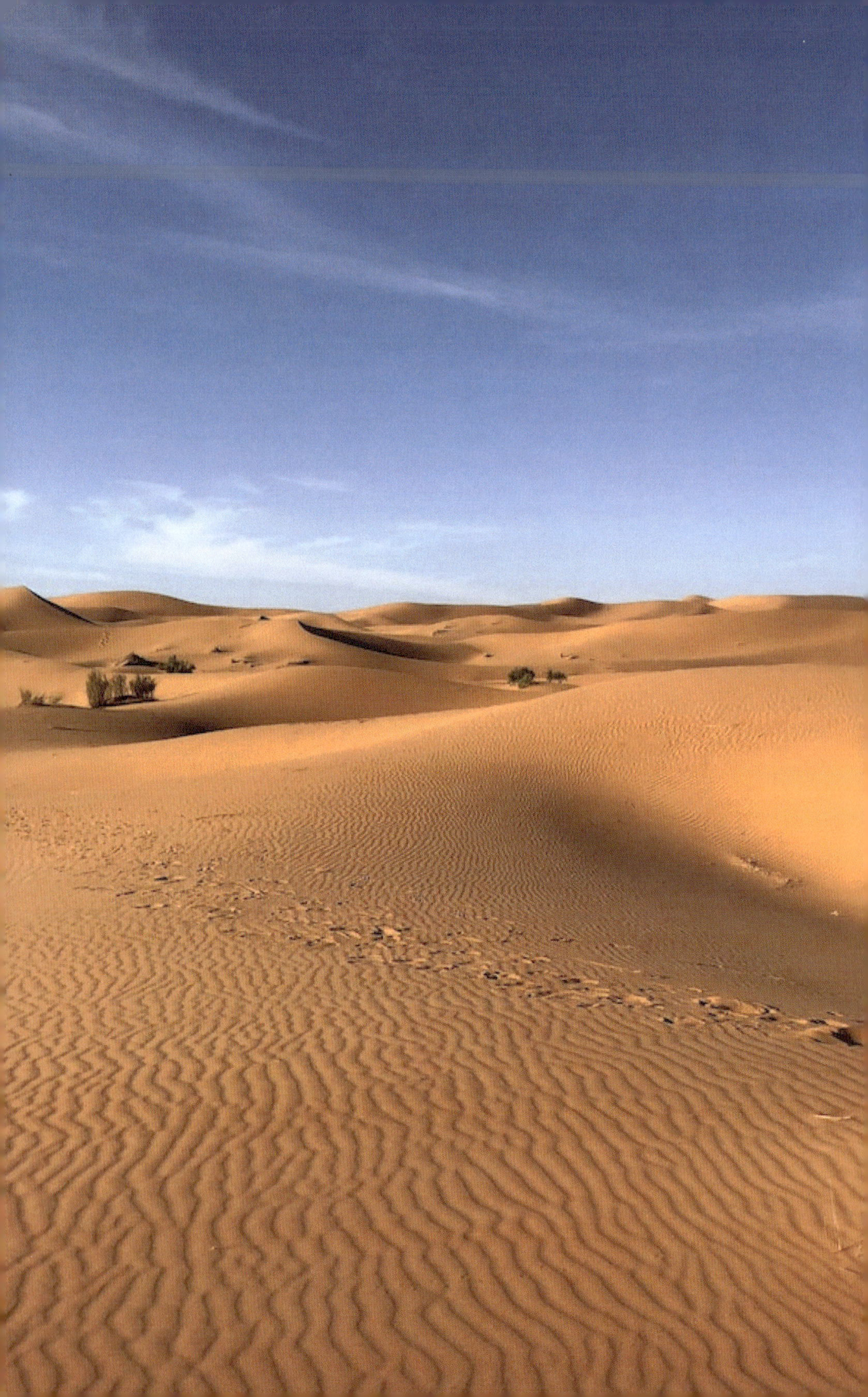

WHERE DO THEY LIVE?

Fennec foxes live in both sandy and semi-arid desert regions in North Africa, throughout the Sahara Desert, and east to Sinai and Arabia.

They have a wide range from Morocco to Egypt, south to northern Niger and Sudan and east to Kuwait.

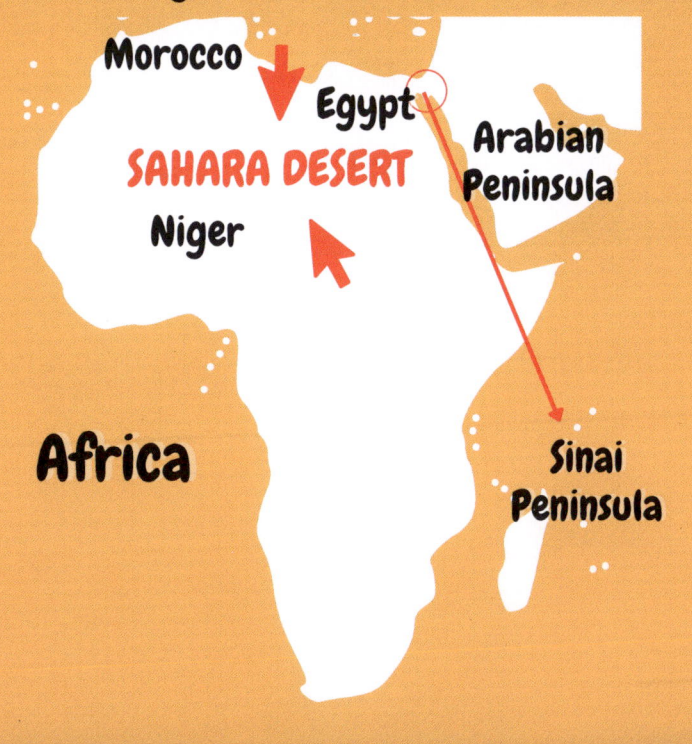

Morocco
Egypt
Arabian Peninsula
SAHARA DESERT
Niger
Africa
Sinai Peninsula

WHAT DO THEY EAT?

Fennec foxes are omnivores as they eat both animal and plant material.

They hunt for small creatures such as insects, small reptiles and rodents in and on the sand.

Grasshopper (insect)

They also eat vegetation such as grasses, roots, berries and fruit.

Did you know?

Like many other desert-living animals, fennec foxes get almost all the **water** they need through the vegetation they eat!

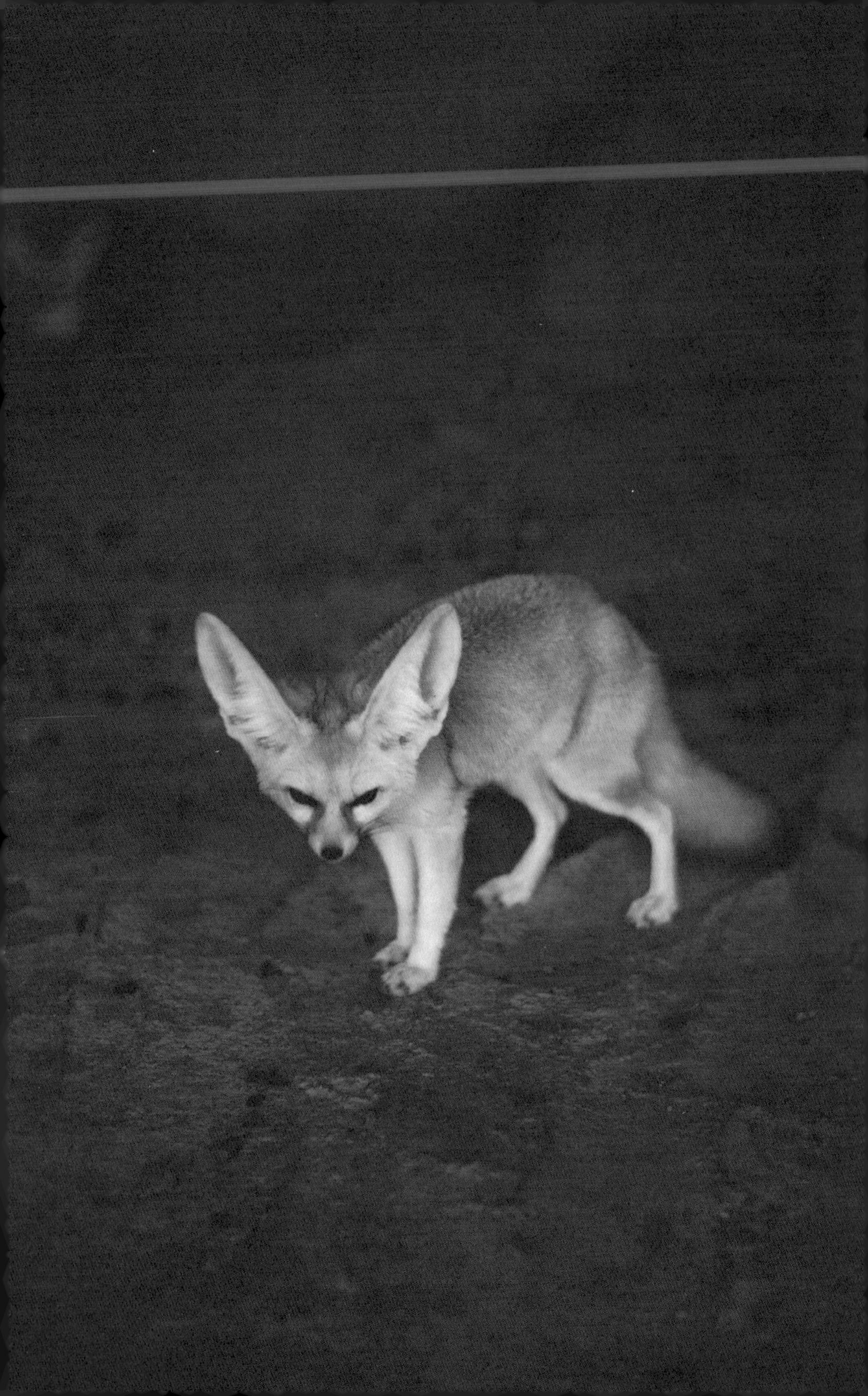

DAILY LIFE

Fennec foxes are largely nocturnal animals that tend to be most active during the cooler nights.

This helps protect them from the African heat and keeps them safe from predators during the day!

They dig extensive underground burrows in the sand where they sleep for most of the day.

LIVING IN THE DESERT

Fennec foxes are well adapted for survival in the heat as well in the cold!

Their fur keeps them <u>warm</u> when desert temperatures fall at night

BUT also keeps them <u>cooler</u> during the hot daytime as the sandy color reflects sunlight.

Fennec foxes sleep curled up with their tail over their nose and feet.

This keeps them warm while they sleep in their underground dens.

Did you know?

The large pointy ears of fennec foxes are not just for show! The ears help these tiny foxes release extra body heat. This **cools off** the foxes during the day.

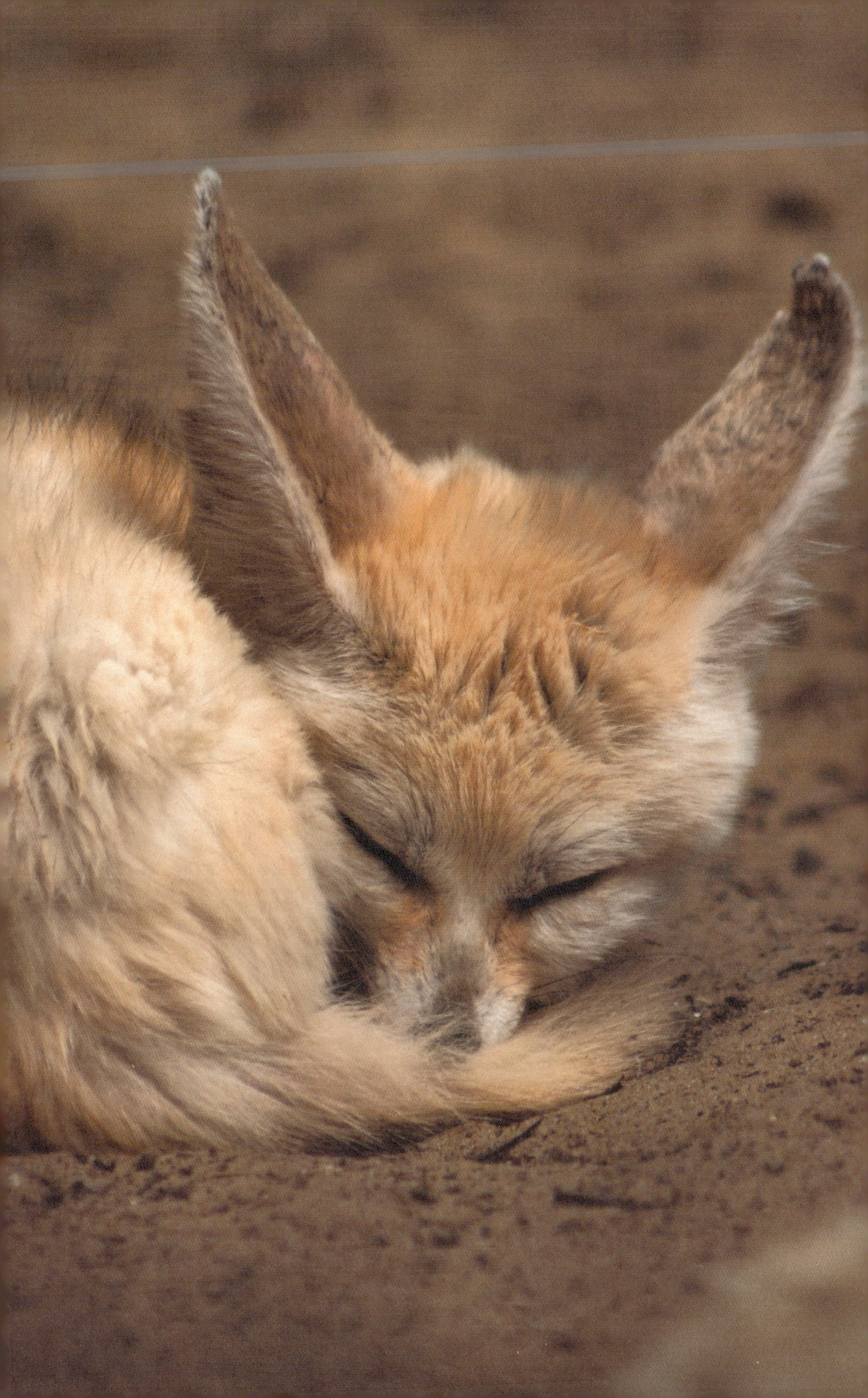

BEHAVIOR

Fennec foxes are UNIQUE among foxes because they are sociable.

While other foxes mostly spend their time alone, fennec foxes live in complex, connected burrows together with up to 10 individuals.

Each fox or pair have their own territory within the underground community!

23

Like other canids, male fennec foxes mark their territory with urine and become very aggressive with each other during the mating season.

Much like other canids, such as red foxes, fennec foxes fight each other over a mate to have babies with.

Red foxes fighting

Fennec foxes have few predators because they are very agile and spend most of their daytime sleeping safely in underground burrows.

Eagle owls are the main predator of the fennec fox.

Giant eagle owl

They are also hunted by larger mammals like hyenas, jackals, caracals, and domestic dogs.

Hyena **Jackal** **Caracal**

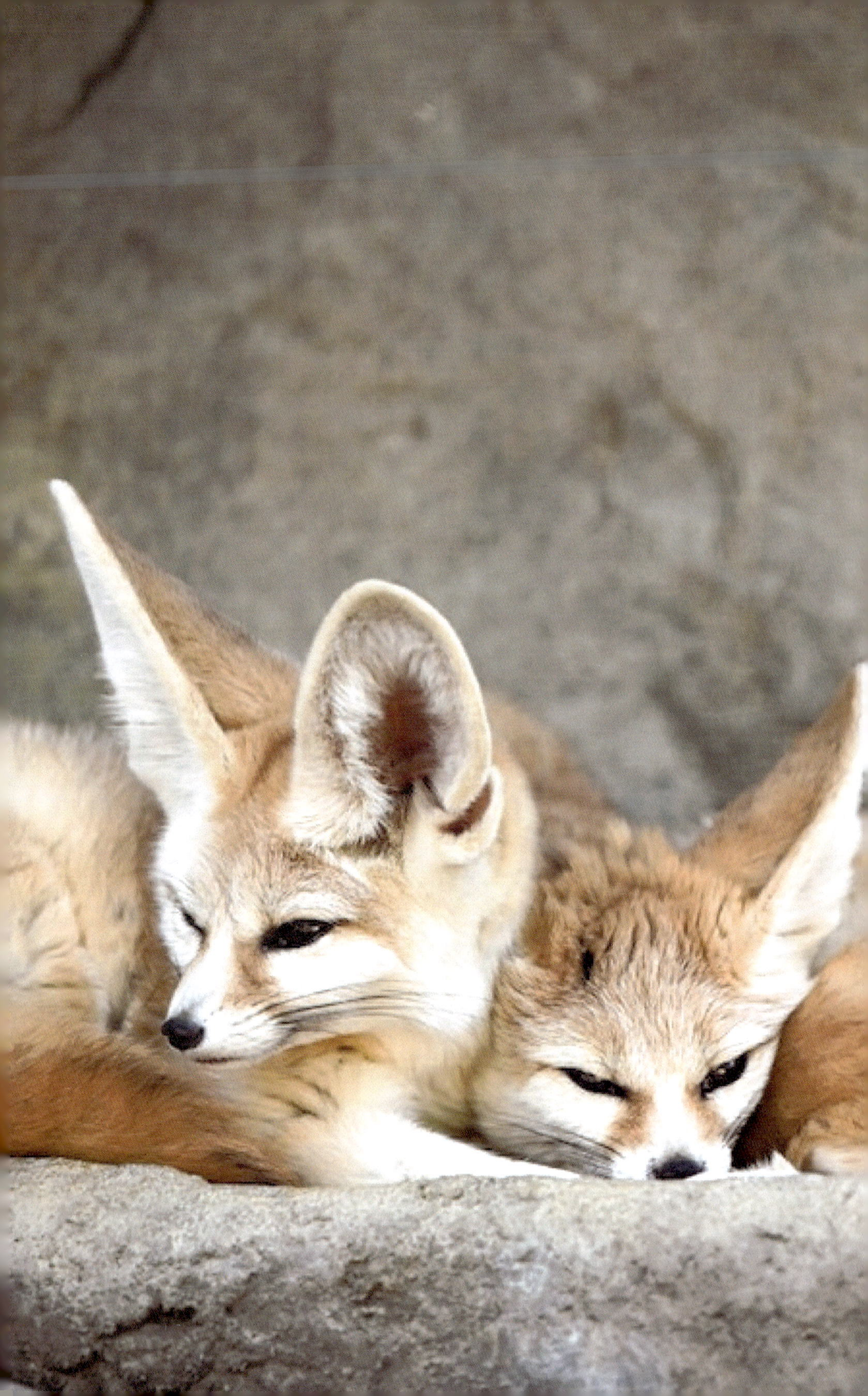

FAMILY LIFE

Fennec foxes mate between January and March. They mate with the SAME partner for life!

Vixens carry their young for 2 months, then give birth to a litter of 2-5 offspring.

The young known as cubs or kits are born with grey skin and weighing just 50 grams at birth.

Photo: courtesy of Chattanooga Zoo.

Young fennec foxes remain in the den with their mother for the first two months of their life.

Fennec foxes are fully mature by the time they are 11 months old.

COMMUNICATION

Fennec foxes are usually very loud, energetic creatures.

Vocalizations among these foxes are common, and are heard as whimpers, barks, shrieks, squeaks, growls, howls or chatters.

INTERESTING FACTS

1

Small fennec fox communities are often called a skulk or a leash.

2

When the heat rises during the day, a fennec fox can take as many as 690 breaths in 60 seconds. This is 30 times faster than its normal breathing!

3

Using their incredibly <u>sensitive hearing</u>, they can hear prey walking around on the soft sand or burrowing into it.

4

The fennec fox is the <u>national animal</u> of Algeria. It also used as a nickname for the Algeria national football team: "Les Fennecs"!

5 The fennec fox can go for long periods without water. This is because their *kidneys* are specially developed to make sure there is minimal water loss in their daily lives.

KIDNEYS - organs that remove water and waste from the blood

LIFESPAN

Fennec foxes are often hunted by locals for their beautiful fur. They are also captured by people to be sold into the exotic pet trade.

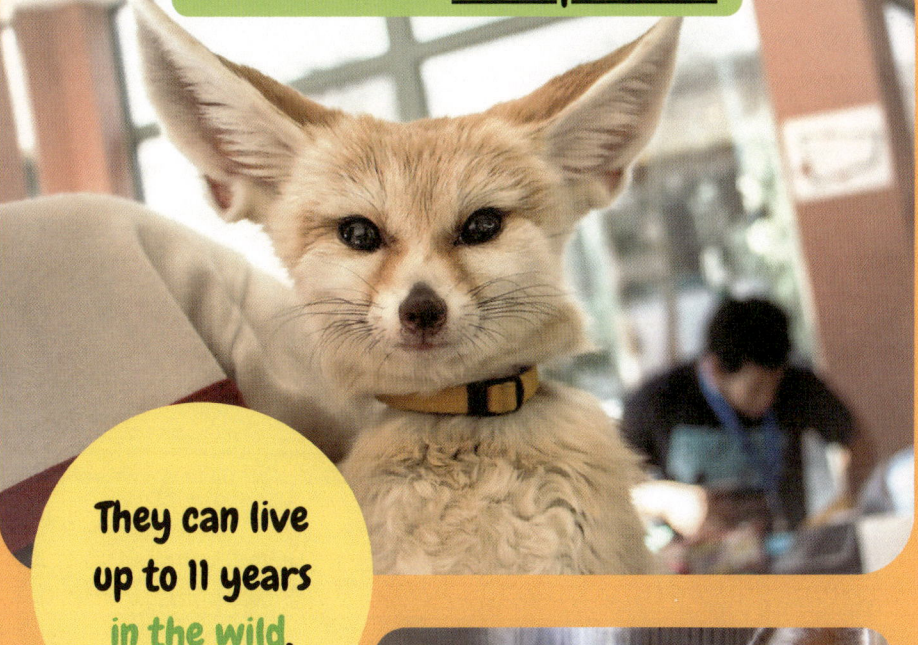

They can live up to 11 years in the wild.

They can live to be 14 years old in captivity.

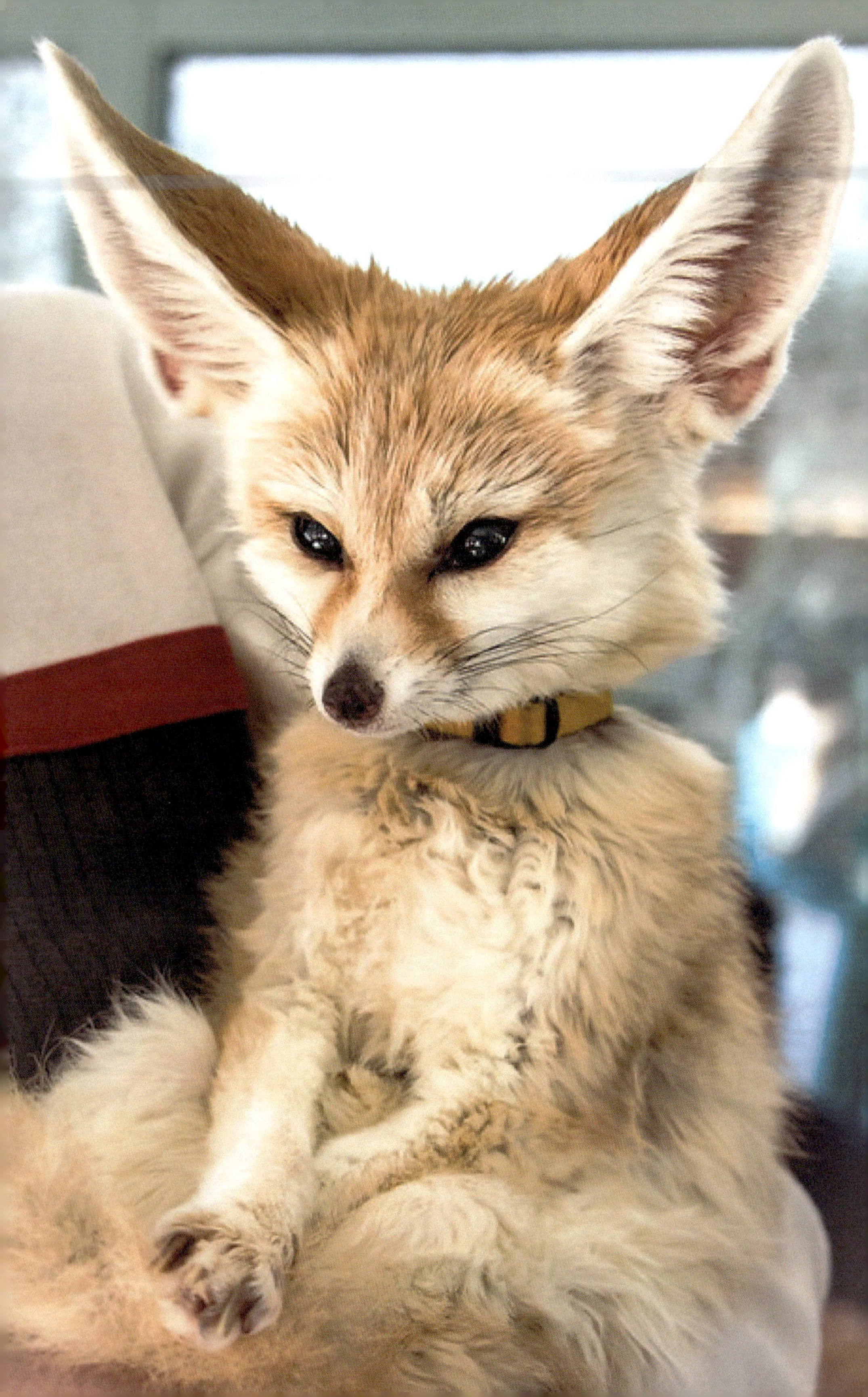

FENNEC FOXES AS PETS

Laws about owning a fennec fox depend on where you live in the world. For example, even among the different states of the United States, the laws vary.

If adopting a fennec fox, it's best that it was born in captivity and not in the wild.

Captive-bred fennec foxes better adapt to life as pets!

While clearly cute, fennec foxes are also very noisy, energetic creatures. Even more so than most dogs!

While they can live with humans, you need to put in a LOT OF WORK to give these big-eared pets the correct types of exercise, diet, and veterinary care!

Fennec foxes need a huge amount of space to explore, climb and play.

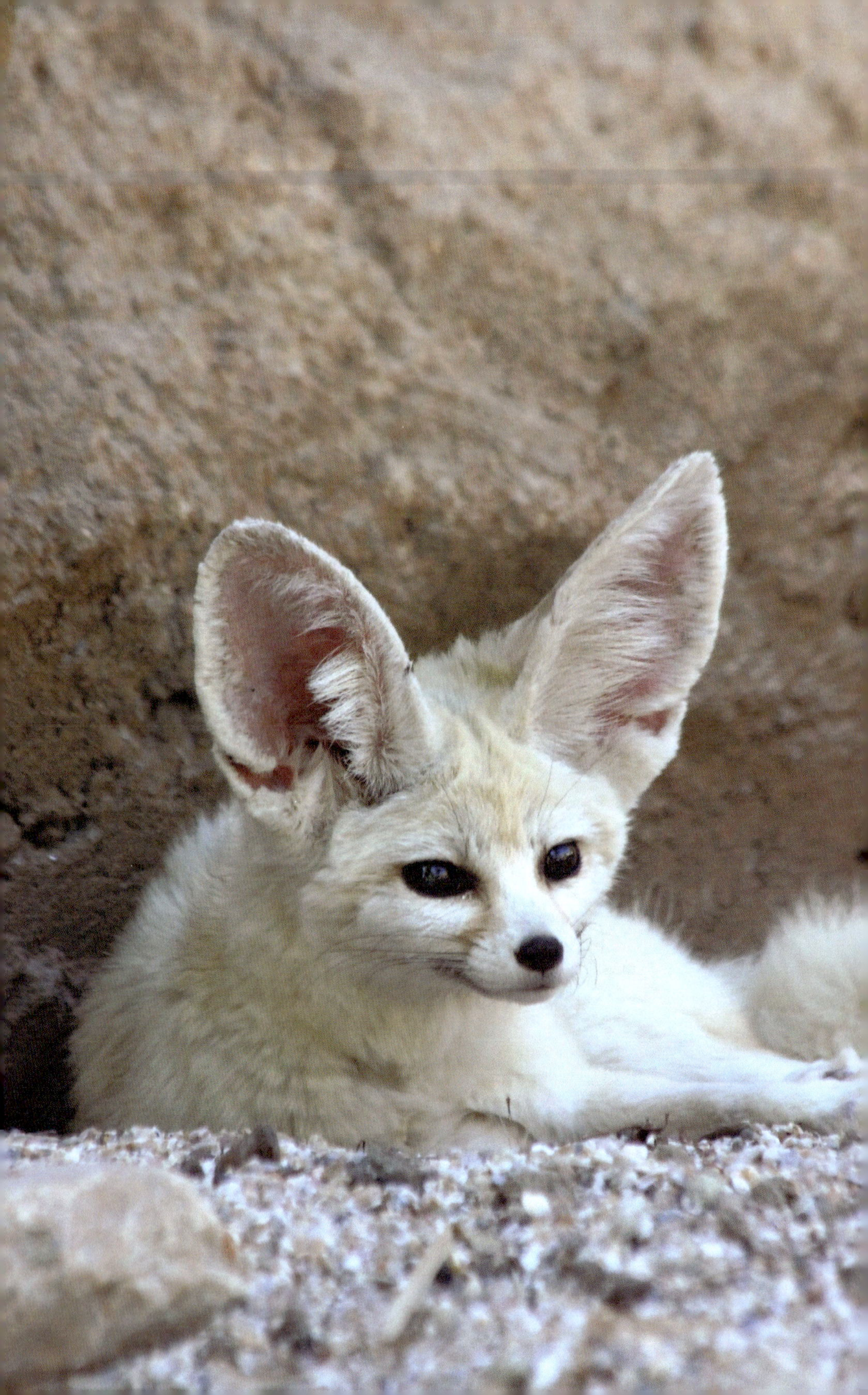

FUTURE OF FENNEC FOXES

The fennec fox is a species of least concern.

Hunting fennec foxes for their fur as well as to be sold as pets is common among locals. Even so, they are not considered threatened, although we don't know how many of them are left in the wild...

Conservation: The fennec fox is protected by law in Morocco, Algeria, Tunisia and Egypt.

QUIZ TIME!

1. Fennec foxes are part of which group?
a) reptiles
b) amphibians
c) birds
d) mammals

2. What are fennec foxes based on diet?
a) carnivores
b) hypercarnivore
c) omnivores
d) herbivores

3. What are male adult foxes called?
a) cubs
b) vixens
c) dogs
d) pumas

4. How many young do arctic foxes have?
a) 1
b) 1-3
c) 2-5
d) 5-10

5. What are fennec foxes best known for?
a) large eyes
b) small nose
c) large ears
d) sharp claws

6. Where do fennec foxes live?
a) in deserts
b) in forests
c) in tundra
d) all of the above

7. What do arctic foxes call home?
a) a barn
b) a den
c) a cave
d) a tree

8. When are fennec foxes mostly active?
a) only at dawn
b) during the day
c) only at sunset
d) at night

9. When is the fennec fox mating season?
a) in spring
b) in summer
c) in autumn
d) in winter

Bonus question:

10. What is a fennec fox community called?
a) a leap
b) a skulk
c) a pride
d) a packs

Did you finish the quiz? Well done!

Don't worry if you didn't know the answer to all of the questions at first.

You can go back and read through the book again to find the missing answers.

Hopefully you had fun reading and learned some new amazing facts about your favourite animal.

P.S.
Just in case you didn't manage to find all the answers in the end, we put them here for you to look up.
ANSWERS: 1.d), 2.c), 3.b), 4.c), 5.c), 6.a), 7.b), 8.d), 9.d), 10.b)

GLOSSARY

adapted: to become used to; adjust

burrows: a hole or tunnel dug by an animal as a hiding place or home

camouflage: a way of hiding something by covering or coloring it so that it looks like its surroundings

canid: an animal of the dog (Canidae) family

conservation: protection of animals and nature from loss, pollution, or waste

den: the resting place of wolves, lions, and other wild animals

habitat: the natural environment of an animal or plant

in captivity: animals that are held by humans and prevented from escaping, for example, in a shelter or zoo

in the wild: animals living free in nature

kidneys: organs that remove water and waste from the blood

kits: name for young foxes; cubs

least concern (animal): animal that there is still plenty left in nature

litter: a group of baby animals born from the same mother at the same time

mammals: animals that have fur and feed their young with milk

mate: to come together to make baby animals

mating season: time of year when a type of animal makes babies

nocturnal (animals): animals most active at night

omnivore: type of animal that eats plants AND animals

predator: an animal that hunts other animals for food

prey: an animal that is hunted or caught for food, usually by another animal

range: an area in which a certain animal travels

reflect: to throw back from a surface

reynards (foxes): adult male of a fennec fox

scientific name (of an animal): a name given to an animal by scientists when they find it in nature for the first time

semi-arid: partially dry

skulk: small fennec fox communities

sociable (animal): known to interact with other individuals

species (of animals): a group of animals that can come together to make babies with each other, but not with animals of other groups (species)

territory: an area taken and protected by an animal

vixens (foxes): adult females of a fennec fox

vocalizations: sounds made with the voice

Congratulations!

You have come to the end of this book.

Thank you for reading this far. Here is an extra photo just for you!

Leave us a review on Amazon if you liked the book! ♥

Printed in Great Britain
by Amazon